Eat Your Anxiety Before it Eats You

5 Super Foods You Must Eat to Eliminate Anxiety

SHAWNA SPARLIN

Also by Shawna Sparlin

Magick of Love: Spells to Attract and Keep a Lover, Heal a Broken Relationship

25 All Natural Cough & Cold Remedies: Homemade Recipes to Relieve the Common Cold

Younger Skin in 30 Days or Less: Every Woman's Guide to Natural Skin Care

Eat Your Anxiety Before it Eats You

5 Super Foods You Must Eat to Eliminate Anxiety

by Shawna Sparlin

Published 2015 by Magick Mom Press

actual persons, either living or dead, is strictly coincidental.

The information provided in this book is for educational purposes only, with information that is general in nature and that is not specific to you, the reader. The contents are intended to assist you and other readers in your personal wellness efforts.

Nothing in this book should be construed as personal advice or diagnosis, and must not be used in this manner. The information in this book should not be considered as complete and does not cover all diseases, ailments, physical conditions, or their treatment. You should consult with your physician regarding the applicability of any information provided herein and before beginning any exercise, weight loss, or health care program.

Authors and sources cited throughout retain the copyright to their respective materials.

Table of Contents

Another book on Anxiety? (An Introduction)

Do you like to watch a lot of TV? Even if your answer is no, chances are, when you go about your day, you encounter TV. It's everywhere—in clinics, in electronic stores, in waiting rooms, in the hospitals, in nail salons and many more places. What's my point? There is something about TV that hints at the state of America, even when no one else seems to be talking about it.

It's no secret that health is a huge topic now. People have sworn off meat, and hundreds, if not thousands, have tried that famous "juice diet" that was the hype a couple of years ago. You can see this trend on TV too in the commercials. What else do you see when you watch your favorite TV series? I see ads, lots and lots of advertisements for medication. Depression, or symptoms linked to depression, anxiety, medication to help you sleep at night, and so forth and so on.

You might never have thought much about it before, but these ads are playing for a reason. Americans need and want help. They're not sleeping at night, and they don't know why. They have fear, nervousness, and sometimes experience feelings and emotions so intense that daily life is severely disrupted. Could it be that all these things have an underlying theme?

I used to believe that little discomforts and small aches and pains were normal. The issues didn't seem, to interfere with my life, so I never spent much time being concerned about my anxiety levels. However, after seeing this trend on TV, I began to wonder if there was more to the picture than what I simply thought I knew.

At this point, I started to keep a more accurate account of my feelings of fear and nervousness. While I knew that my anxiety levels weren't to a point of needing medication, I wondered if I was doing myself a disservice by ignoring them as well.

So I decided to do some research, and what I found shocked me. When I discovered this information, I knew I had to share it with someone. I started with my friends and family. But then I thought, "Why stop there?" And so the idea for this book was born.

I've written it especially for you, my reader. I want it to educate and teach you. So many Americans believe that their pain, depression, or anxiety is just a normal course of life. I used to think that way, but not anymore. Over 70% of Americans suffer from some type of anxiety symptom daily; many of them don't even know it.

Can you imagine that? It's not that the symptom is so minor that they live fine lives, but rather they've become so accustomed to the symptom that they consider it normal when it's not. That means over half of Americans are settling simply because they don't know they can do something about it. Now that I've done the research, I've compiled it all here for you. I want your eyes to be opened and for you to know and understand the truth.

You don't have to live with anxiety—not if you're willing to do something about it and take action. If you're not sure you even have a problem with anxiety, I urge you to continue reading this book. If not for your sake, perhaps for the sake of someone else that you know. Educate yourself so that you can teach them.

I believe everyone deserves a chance at a fulfilling life. The information contained in this book isn't a guide to all your health concerns and issues, but to one aspect of it specifically: anxiety. If you or someone you know struggles with anxiety, this book is just what you need to learn the truth. Keep reading to discover what I've learned.

Anxiety: What it is and isn't

Have you ever had to get in front of a group of people, friends even, and talk about something? Public speaking is a huge "fear" that many people have. In fact, it's so common that people find themselves uncomfortable with the idea of speaking in front of an audience, that many high schools and virtually every college requires you take a class on the subject.

When you take a class on public speaking, you find that a lot of things you feel internally when faced with public speaking are normal. It's called presentation anxiety. Because a lot of the symptoms for severe anxiety issues are the same for a normal response, it's hard to determine when you're dealing with something that's more than normal.

Anxiety is the human body's physiological response to threatening stimuli. When we encounter something that scares us, we respond on two different levels: mentally and physically. A physiological response is our bodies' physical response to what scares us.

The response isn't meant to debilitate us, but to amp us up and get us ready to fight or flight. Have you ever heard of this response in the human body? It's caused by the rush of adrenaline released into our bodies when we feel threatened or scared. That release of adrenaline speeds our heart rate; increases our breathing and gives us the ability to lift a car (not over our heads) but high enough to free a stuck kid.

It's that rush of adrenaline which allows us to outrun danger if need be. To climb trees to escape wild animals. I know what you're thinking. But public speaking doesn't involve any of that. You're absolutely right. It doesn't. But our bodies still respond the same way. In the same sense, that extra rush of adrenaline can give us the ability to stand and deliver a killer message. The adrenaline can make us confident and sure of ourselves.

That's the normal response. We feel the butterflies and tightening in our gut, and we push through it and beyond, giving powerful speeches, presentations, standing up for ourselves, or confronting a scary person. We can accomplish these things because of the fight or flight response our bodies kick into automatically. It's a good and natural response to outside "threatening" stimuli.

I've mentioned all of this because I want you to understand that anxiety is normal. Just because you worry about your annual or quarterly review at work doesn't mean you have a problem. If your children's grades are suffering at school and it causes you fear and concern, then you will have responded like most parents. These are all normal.

Life gets difficult at times—and that's an understatement! Many people experience great loss and sorrow and circumstances so severe it can seem like there is no hope or way out. Each of these things are processed mentally and physically. You'll also be challenged mentally and physically. Again, this is all normal. You can easily determine when it's more than just normal concerns and reasonable responses to emotional times in your life by utilizing the following markers we'll cover in the next chapter.

Anxiety Symptoms: When it's more than just worry

Andrea paced the wooden floors of her bedroom quickly. Her mind raced, thinking about the letter she had just received. It was already starting. After her husband suffered a chronic heart attack last fall, they were never able to recover. Him physically, her financially. They had always worked together to make their income cover their expenses and bills, but with him out of work for failing health, it just wasn't going to be enough.

They had talked about life insurance but had never made anything concrete out of it—the prices were just too high. Now she regretted it. She would have done anything to go back and make up the extra money it would have taken to secure her future financially now.

Creditors had started calling her all last week. She was constantly receiving email notifications of new alerts being added to her credit report each month. Late payments here, an account in default there. She couldn't take it anymore. She hadn't even been able to afford a decent burial for Mark, her now deceased husband.

She had a lot of anger towards him. He could have survived if he wanted to, but he didn't fight for them—for her. Now she was in a world of financial hurt, and she had no idea how she was going to get out…

~*~

As I mentioned in the last chapter, situations like this, however unfortunate, happen all the time. People experience something they weren't prepared for and worry how they'll pull through. This fear and worry might come back a couple of times a week or several times a month. If the situation is desperate, your circumstance won't be far from your mind. The huge question is: When does it become something more?

According to Health.com, PsychCentral.com, and WebMD, the simple difference between normal worry and anxiety and debilitating anxiety disorders is when the distress interferes with your ability to have a normal life. We'll define normal in the following paragraphs:

Consider the short story at the beginning of this chapter. Andrea is faced with some serious issues. Whether or not her anxiety becomes debilitating determines how she reacts to what she has experienced in her life.

Normal Response

• She experiences feelings of anger but can make calls to agencies, friends, and family, asking for help

• She realizes that her fears and worries are natural. Her situation is terrible, but she doesn't dwell on them day in and day out

• She is severely distressed, as her situation is bad, but she continues to take action each day to fix her situation; even if they're small, baby steps

• Under normal, non-extenuating circumstances, significant worrying wouldn't last long, but for brief periods. In a situation as intense as Andrea's, some physiological symptoms might occur (such as issues sleeping at night, irritability, muscle soreness, fatigue, etc.)

Abnormal "Excessive" Response

• Her situation interferes with job performance and social life. She can no longer focus while at work and fails to return calls from friends or family.

• She could not shake the sense that her situation is outside her control and that it would not ever end, even if she wanted it to. Her fears and worries invade every aspect of her life

• Under normal, non-extenuating circumstances worry or mounting stress come from unknown sources; suddenly, there is just fear, worry, and concern that cannot be stopped

• Under non-extenuating circumstances, these problems and issues can be traced to having lasted for at least six months

• Under non-extenuating circumstances, the stress, worry, and concern is accompanied with sleep issues, muscle aches and soreness, body tenderness, fatigue or restlessness, and more

I made sure to include a pretty dramatic situation because sometimes, when life throws us curve balls such as Andrea's situation, it can be difficult. In a situation that tough, you can expect to experience worry and physiological issues for an extended period of time. However, under normal circumstances, worry and pressure shouldn't be so great that your body responds with fatigue, body soreness and other physical ailments.

When issues get bad, as in individuals suffering from anxiety that prevents them from living healthy lives, they experience other disorders. I have a few listed below:

Generalized Anxiety Disorder

This disorder is a chronic anxiety illness that can be identified by extremely long periods of excessive worry, high anxiety, and distress about unknown, nonspecific circumstances and life events. Someone suffering from this very real disorder will find themselves worrying about everything you can imagine in life: kids, work, money; anything. Even if there is nothing to really worry about. Everything is a cause for worry no matter how illogical or unreasonable.

Panic Disorder

Many people have likely heard of the term "panic attack". It's an occurrence that many people describe as a sudden onset of terror, dread, and apprehension. These feelings of darkness and uncertainty can cause the body to shake uncontrollably, cause nausea, and trouble breathing. They can be as short as a minute or as long as 10. Some people have even experienced them for longer periods of time.

Once someone experiences a panic attack, apprehension about the event can plague them. It's not uncommon for someone who experienced a long, terrifying panic attack to adopt behaviors to prevent them in the future, which inadvertently makes them worry about their reoccurring panic attacks.

Phobia

While many people have heard of a phobia at one point in time in their life, I believe few people take the time to consider the people that are affected by this disorder daily. Phobias are irrational fears concerning situations, objects, things and people. It becomes a phobia when the person can acknowledge the fear as irrational, but they are powerless to stop themselves from reacting to it.

Social Anxiety Disorder

This type of anxiety disorder is born of a deep fear of being seen or judged negatively by others, even strangers. This disorder is also characterized by a high degree of fear concerning public embarrassment as a result of irrational, rash actions. Someone suffering from this would never get on a stage and have trouble relating to someone intimately because of their deep fear. In extreme cases, it can cause the one suffering to go to great lengths to avoid people, public situations, and even human contact.

The Rest of the Population

While there are certainly other debilitating anxieties out there, these are the more common ones people often tend to associate with the general realm of anxiety disorders. Individuals suffering from these disorders need serious medical intervention to help them lead normal, healthy everyday lives. The good news is that for everyone else, there are ways that you can help your body deal with the way it responds to stress and anxiety.

Common methods of reducing anxiety and stress involve simple education. Some people get worked up about anxiety because they wonder if it's normal. Yes! It's normal and to be expected throughout life. Other people feel extreme stress because of their financial situation, work situation, children, life events such as death, divorces, miscarriages, and so on. For these other people that encounter serious life events, there are ways to cope with the stress.

Remember how I said you respond to anxiety and outside threatening stimuli in two different ways? Many people will say that they cannot help the way their bodies respond to outside stress. This book will help you see that you can change the way your body reacts to stress. In fact, you can change your body's ability to handle stress to such a degree that you can virtually erase the extreme anxiety you feel in your life. First, you need to make sure you STOP practicing the following behaviors:

MOPING – Bad things in life happen, and they happen to good, well-meaning people. In order to gain control of your anxiety, you need to take action. Don't just mope. Spending time by yourself in solitude with the lights off, and a bottle of alcohol isn't going to make your reality any less real.

DISASTER THINKING – This is just what it sounds like. There is no positive to your thoughts. You don't think your life can go on anymore. You've hit the bottom, and all, you see, is darkness. You rationalize continuing to mope because all the avenues you see in front of you seem useless. They won't work out so why even try? Disaster thinking leads to an attitude of more hopelessness and inability to take action regarding your situation.

DISBELIEF – If you've encountered an intense life event, stop saying, "I can't believe it." Unfortunately, if you want to move forward, you're going to have to believe it. It happened, whatever it was, however bad and unfortunate. It isn't right—not fair; but, it doesn't matter. What matters now is the action you take to move forward and out of the terrible event. This doesn't mean that you ignore it or pretend that it didn't happen. That's disbelief. I'm talking about learning to accept what has happened. It's a part of who you are now, a part of your past and a part of your story. Accept it, and move forward with action.

These three actions alone can help reduce how you respond to serious stimuli in your life. However, if you want to eradicate stress completely from your life, you'll have to take even more dramatic moves. I'm talking about a complete lifestyle change. Join me in the next chapter to find out how changing the types of foods you eat can help you accomplish this.

The Secret to Erasing Your Anxiety

Believe it or not, your diet plays a very important part to how you respond mentally and physically to anxiety. Are you a heavy caffeine drinker? What about refined and processed foods? Do you love fast foods, deep fried meat, and processed sugars? All these "foods" affect the hormone levels in your body.

No, they are not the source of your anxiety, as in you're not going to be super stressed for an exam because you ate a fast food hamburger. However, they can make it worse, causing fatigue and aiding in your ability to concentrate to do what is necessary to take action and push through your circumstance.

How is this possible? Consider foods that are rich in caffeine, like coffee, sodas, and energy drinks, etc. Caffeine is a stimulant and can cause your heart to race and feelings of restlessness, jitters, and sweaty palms. These feelings can exacerbate the anxiety you already feel. Also, caffeine reacts with chemicals in your body that can cause your adrenal gland (the one responsible for releasing adrenaline) to excrete stress hormones even when you don't need them. Too will make you feel even more anxious.

And that's just caffeine! Turns out, there're tons of different ways to give your body the ability to handle stress better. For the purposes of this book, I've chosen five incredible anxiety-reducing super foods.

If you infuse these foods into your diet, you'll find that not only will you feel better, but you'll be able to handle anxiety better as well.

Blueberries

Did you know these little berries have been found to lower anxiety in patients in as little as a month and a half or six weeks? When you're stressed, your body consumes massive amounts of Vitamin C to protect and repair cell health. Blueberries are rich in Vitamin C and antioxidants which help fight off free radicals within your body.

Free radicals are a danger to your body because they roam, attacking stable molecules at their core structure. Antioxidants can stabilize the free radicals and keep them from weakening important cells your body needs to maintain optimum levels of health.

They also play a significant role in lowering your blood sugar. When your blood sugar levels are imbalanced, they can disrupt the neurotransmitters your brain releases. Neurotransmitters are chemicals released at nerve endings to be received across the synapse (space in between one nerve ending and the beginning of another) into the receptor sites. When these chemicals are not released in their proper proportions, they can cause anxiety symptoms, depression, and more.

Turkey

Many people understand turkey as a sleep aid. That's why everyone's always so tired after Thanksgiving Day! However, turkey isn't just for the holidays! The tryptophan found in turkey, a chemical that can cause drowsiness, also helps the body release serotonin when ingested. Serotonin has a nickname of the "feel good" chemical. It's a mood lifter like the beta-endorphin released by your body when you exercise.

Turkey also contains a rich source of proteins and B vitamins. When your body is deficient in B vitamins, your body is unable to release the right amount of neurotransmitters to regulate your mood properly. Depression and anxiety have a common linking because one often proceeds from the other. Again, free-range organic turkey is the best choice, as commercially mass-produced turkey varieties in most local grocers will tend to be stock full of hormones that will also affect you, and most likely for worse.

Spinach

Organic spinach is full of magnesium, a mineral that can regulate the cortisol or stress hormone, within your body. Healthy levels of cortisol will leave you feeling happy. Too much or too little and you'll struggle with weight gain, anxiety, and depression. It's also a rich supplier of folate, the natural form of folic acid that is used in most supplements. Several different studies have been able to link low levels of folate successfully to depression and anxiety.

Almonds

More than just a nut, it can be found in a rich, fatty delicious butter now too. They're packed full of protein and also present a great food for healthy doses of magnesium and calcium. These two minerals work together to support healthy function of your nervous system. This bodily system regulates different bodily functions which can affect the way your body responds to stress and outside stimuli.

Rich in Vitamin B2, and other minerals like potassium, zinc, and iron, almonds are great for mood regulation. Raw, uncooked almonds are the best. They're also pretty easy to slip into your diet. Try sliced almonds in cereals or mixed in with yogurt. Top your salads with them—anything to give your body more of what it needs. You'll likely feel a difference is as little as 30 days or less!

Salmon

Fish. Many women understand fish to be avoided during pregnancy because of high mercury content and even more so now due to rising levels of pollution in the seas. However, freshwater salmon is known primarily for its rich omega-3 fatty acids. You've likely heard of omega-3s before, but what exactly do you know about them?

For starters, they help keep cortisol in check along with your adrenaline. This means that even when you encounter stress, omega-3 fatty acids can keep these two stress hormones from spiking. High levels of these two hormones cause extreme physical symptoms such as shakiness, restlessness, and a racing heartbeat. They also provide you with great heart protection too and are recommended to fight plaque and fat buildup in your arteries.

Delicious Recipes for All Times of the Day!

It's easy to throw blueberries and almonds into a salad and call it a day. The truth is that you'll need a lot more than that on a regular basis if you're looking to eradicate anxiety in your life. Because of that, I've included recipes for each of these foods for breakfast, lunch, dinner, dessert time, and even for snacks. Eat turkey for breakfast?! That's right, salmon too.

Some of these recipes are quick and easy, while others will take a good bit to prepare. Either way, your health is worth it! If you're looking to get serious about taking control of the anxiety in your life, consider stocking up on some of these ingredients and trying them out. Your mouth will love you for it, and your body will thank you too!

Blueberries

Breakfast

When it comes to berries, breakfast muffins, scones, and delicious sweet cakes, come to mind. The only problem with this is that in the real world, people don't have 30 minutes to an hour in the morning to prepare such a delicious warm treat. As I stated earlier, these foods don't do much for you unless their pure, natural, and organic. That rules out fast food breakfast munchies and the delectable bakery specials from your local food stores.

Under normal circumstances, you might be in a bind, but where there's a will, there's a way. When buying blueberries, your local farmer's market is best. You can freeze them, eat them alone, or throw them into some ice cream on a hot day. Try infusing your breakfast routine with these little guys, I've got a couple of recipes that take less than 20 minutes to make from prep to finish! Breakfast isn't the only meal these berries can be used to make. You can toss some in salads, like the Blueberry Mexican Salad with Avocado recipe below, and even use them to top your beefy concoctions with as you'll see in the Blueberry Flambé with Beef and Brandy.

Blueberry Oatmeal Smoothie – Chilled and Delicious

Prep Time: 1 min

Cook Time: 1 min

I can't leave the breakfast section for blueberries without mentioning a great delicious blueberry smoothie! This one tastes just like a cup of creamy oats with a little tang! It's ready as soon as you get your ingredients together and toss them in the blender—perfect for those with super busy lifestyles!

Ingredients:

1 C water

1 C almond milk

½ C organic oats

1 C organic blueberries

1-2 Tbsps. organic, unsalted, butter (try it with almond butter!)

1 banana

Cinnamon, to taste

Combine ingredients minus cinnamon in a blender cup and liquefy! Or, blend until your desired consistency has been reached. Sometimes I like to blend with ice, or with frozen blueberries. You can do both, ice, and frozen blueberries. Or you can keep the ice and use fresh blueberries (which are totally delicious too). With this quickie recipe, the choice is all yours! Sprinkle with cinnamon to taste and enjoy as you head out the door!

Blueberry Banana Nut Oatmeal – Hot and Ready!

Prep Time: 3 min

Cook Time: 5 min

This recipe takes a little twist from traditional blueberry/cereal combinations. You're sure to become a fan of hot cereal when you try this for the first time!

Ingredients:

½ C old fashioned oats

½ C water

½ C milk (try it with almond milk)

1 Sm banana sliced to your preference

1 Tbsp. brown sugar

½ Tsp vanilla

¼ C freshly washed blueberries

1 Tbsp. chopped almonds

Combine the water and milk with the oats and half of the banana sliced to your preference into a saucepan on medium heat. Let the mixture cook until the oats start to bubble, and then stir until oats are done cooking. They'll be nice and creamy, about 3 minutes more. Remove your pan from heat and mix in the brown sugar with vanilla. Now you're ready to eat! Pour your delicious breakfast into a bowl and top with the remaining almonds, blueberries and banana slices.

Lunch

Blueberries with Curried Wheat berries

Prep Time: 25 min

Cook Time: 65 min

This delicious salad of blueberries and wheat berries can be room temperature or served chilled. It's healthy and hearty. The Indian curry flavor of the nutty wheat berries mixes with the sweet blueberries to give your mouth a taste it won't soon forget.

Ingredients:

1 ½ C hard wheat berries, rinsed and picked over

½ tsp. ground turmeric

2 tsp. salt

¼ C fresh lemon juice

2 cloves garlic, minced

1 tsp. grated ginger root (fresh is best)

4 tsp curry powder

1 ½ Tsp Vinaigrette (to garnish, optional)

¾ C canola oil

½ C cilantro, loosely chopped

2 C Blueberries

½ C almonds, raw or toasted

3 scallions (total, thinly sliced on diagonal)

¼ C mint, loosely chopped

Ground black pepper to taste

Combine the wheat berries, turmeric and salt with water in a large pot over high heat. Mixture should be covered with at least 2 inches of water. Bring to a boil and then reduce to simmer for 55 to 65 more minutes. Cook uncovered until wheat berries are soft, tender, and ready. Drain and let stand to cool.

While the wheat berries cook, make the curry vinaigrette by combining the lemon juice, garlic, ginger and curry powder into a bowl. Whisk oil in slowly and add the cilantro. Your vinaigrette is ready. Set aside and wait for wheat berries to finish.

To prepare salad, stir in vinaigrette to moisten the warm wheat berries thoroughly. Add in blueberries, almonds, scallions and mint. Toss gently while adding more salt, vinaigrette, and black pepper to taste.

Blueberry Mexican Salad with Avocado

Prep Time: 15 min

Cook Time: 20 min

You won't need a different dressing for this recipe as the creamy avocado will suffice. Use a ripe, organic avocado so that it'll mix well and break down as you toss your salad during preparation.

Ingredients:

1 ½ C corn kernels (cut from 3 corn cobs)

2 tsp olive oil

4 C shredded romaine (about 6 ounces)

1 package (6 oz. or ¼ C) blueberries

1 C (½ in cubes) jicama

1 ripe, diced avocado

½ C cilantro leaves, chopped

2 Tbsps. lime juice

½ tsp salt, to taste

Preheat oven to 400°F. In medium bowl, combine the corn with olive oil and toss, coating thoroughly. Spread this mixture evenly onto a rimmed baking pan coated or lined with parchment paper to prevent sticking. Roast in over for 25 minutes.

Remove the pan from the oven and mix the corn, ending by spreading it back out on the pan. Roast again for another 5 to 10 minutes, or until at least half reach a deep brown hue. Remove and let cool.

While the corn is roasting, take a large bowl and toss the remaining ingredients until blended evenly. Salt and season to taste. When corn is roasted, add to mixture and toss some more to coat. Serve immediately. This doesn't save very well (as you can imagine) so don't plan on leftovers.

Dinner

Blueberry Flambé with Beef and Brandy

Prep Time: 5 min

Cook Time: 51 min

This flambé can be used with any grilled beef. The sweetness of the blueberries, butter and sugar, is accented with the brandy and thyme. You're going to want to make this one more than once!

Ingredients:

1 ½ to 2 lbs. beef (or 4 steaks)

Pinch olive oil

Pinch of salt and black pepper

2 cloves garlic cloves, crushed with a press

12 oz. blueberries

2 Tbsps. butter

2 Tbsps. fresh thyme leaves

2 tsp sugar

¼ C brandy (your favorite brand)

Rinse the beef with water, pat dry and then rub with oil, salt, pepper and garlic. Cook on a grill, and then let stand 5 minutes. Slice meat if desired, but not necessary. Keep warm while you prepare the flambé.

Combine 6 oz. of blueberries with butter, thyme, and sugar into a skillet or saucepan. Cook over medium-high heat for about 2 to 3 minutes. Pop the blueberries while you cook and stir to release their juice. Let the sauce thicken.

When sauce starts to thicken, add the remaining berries and reduce heat, bringing down to a simmer. Add the brandy and then remove from heat. Immediately light the sauce. Use a long handle match or lighter. While still lit, swirl the sauce and pour over meat while flames die down. Serve warm.

Grilled Blueberry Salmon

Prep Time: 15 min

Cook Time: 30 min total time 45 min

This recipe calls for two of our super foods to create an incredible taste you'll crave again and again. The sweet blueberry combined with the taste of the freshwater salmon is unique and flavorful!

Ingredients:

1 ¼ lbs. salmon fillets (cut to your preference)

½ tsp salt

½ tsp pepper

1/3 C fresh blueberries

1/3 C ketchup

1 Tbsp. apple cider vinegar

1 Tbsp. balsamic vinegar (try it with blueberry flavor)

2 Tbsps. brown sugar

¼ tsp garlic powder

½ tsp onion powder

½ tsp ground mustard

1 tsp Worcestershire sauce

Begin by heating a medium to small saucepan on low heat with blueberries. Cook until berries pop, about 10 minutes. Mash with a fork. Combine with both vinegars, ketchup, brown sugar, onion and remaining spices minus salt and pepper. Whisk together to break down blueberries. When thoroughly mixed, turn up the heat to medium. Let the sauce bubble before turning back down to a simmer for 20 minutes, whisking periodically to keep from burning or sticking to the pan. When finished, your sauce will be thick and clumpier than regular BBQ sauce. Cover and let stand.

For the meat, preheat grill to highest setting. Season your salmon with salt and pepper, and once the grill is ready, lay filets centered on top. Cook for 5 minutes, then flip. Coat the salmon with sauce and continue to let cook until flaky and opaque, roughly 5 or 6 minutes more. Once the salmon is done, pour on remaining sauce. Serve and enjoy.

Snacks and Desserts

Glazed Lemon Blueberry Scones

Prep Time: 10 min

Cook Time: 17 - 20 min

Yes, they take a little bit of time, but you'll marvel at the fact that you made them yourself and that they taste so good. The perfect combination of berry, citrus, and glaze, they're great for breakfast, brunch, or dessert.

Ingredients:

2 C flour

¼ C sugar

1 Tbsp baking powder

½ tsp salt

6 Tbsps. butter

½ C milk (Try it with almond milk!)

¼ C lemon juice

2 Tbsps. lemon zest

Dash of vanilla

1 C blueberries

Glaze:

½ C powder sugar

1 Tbsp. lemon juice

Pinch of lemon zest

Preheat oven to 400°. In a bowl combine flour, sugar, baking powder, and salt. Cut cold butter into tiny pieces and place on top of the dry ingredients. It needs to stay cold so that the batter mixes just right. Mix the butter and dry ingredients together. It'll take some time. If using a machine, you'll need to work your way to medium speed. Go slow. Stop as needed to break mixture apart or stir as needed. When butter has broken down into the mixture, stir in milk, lemon juice and lemon zest until moistened.

Dust a clean counter top or cutting board with flour. Pat the dough out and fold blueberries into the dough. Be careful not to squish them and keep them from bleeding.

Next, pat the dough out into a rectangle with your hands. Keep it about an inch thick. Cut once down the middle to create two squares and then diagonally twice to form a crisscross in each square. You should have eight pieces total.

Place the triangle scones onto a cookie sheet about two inches apart. Bake for about 17 minutes or until golden brown. Cool and then drizzle with glaze. Let stand again for glaze to harden.

TO MAKE THE GLAZE: Combine glaze ingredients into a small bowl. Add a little more (or less) lemon juice in order to get the consistency you need. When ready, use a small spoon to drizzle over cooked scones.

Blueberry Sweet Cake

Prep Time: 15 min

Cook Time: 35 – 45 min

This recipe doesn't need much prefacing. The title says it all. Just remember to take it easy on the sweets, as they'll combine with the natural sugars in the blueberries.

Ingredients:

½ C unsalted butter, room temperature

2 tsp lemon zest

¾ C+ 4 Tbsps. sugar (natural, unrefined; leave 1 Tbsp. to sprinkle on top)

1 egg, room temperature

1 tsp vanilla

2 C flour (set aside ¼ C to toss with blueberries)

2 tsp baking powder

1 tsp kosher salt

2 C fresh blueberries

½ C buttermilk***

** This 1 tablespoon is for sprinkling on top

*** Homemade buttermilk: Take1 Tbsp. of vinegar or lemon juice and place in a tall liquid measuring cup.

Add milk until it reaches 1-cup line. Let stand for five minutes. Use ½ C of mixture for recipe.

Preheat the oven to 350ºF. Cream the butter with the lemon zest and ¾ C + 3 Tbsps. sugar until light and fluffy. Add egg and vanilla. Beat until well combined. Toss blueberries with ¼ C of flour. Set aside and then whisk together the remaining flour, baking powder, and salt. Add the flour mixture to the batter slowly, alternating with the buttermilk. Fold in the blueberries gently to prevent bleeding.

Grease a bread-baking pan with butter to prevent sticking. Spread batter in pan. Sprinkle the batter top with remaining Tbsp. of sugar. Bake for 35 to 45 minutes. Check with a toothpick for doneness. Should be clean with no batter sticking to the wood. If needed, bake for a little longer. Let stand to cool at least 15 minutes before serving.

Turkey

Breakfast

Turkey Breakfast Sandwiches

Prep Time: 5 min

Cook Time: 5 min

Again, not just for the holidays! Use leftover turkey from dinner or purchase a small turkey breast for this recipe.

Ingredients:

Biscuits, buns or dinner rolls toast/English muffins!)

Cranberry sauce

Warm mashed potatoes

Warm turkey

Poached, fried or scrambled eggs

Spread the biscuit with a layer of cranberry sauce, and then spoon potatoes top. Add a slice of turkey topped with egg cooked to your preference. Enjoy!

Turkey Hash

Prep Time: 15 min

Cook Time: 25 min

If you like turkey at all times of the year, consider using this recipe that incorporates all of the traditional favorites in one meal.

Ingredients:

1 Tbsp. unsalted butter

½ C yellow onion, chopped

2 large garlic cloves, minced

½ C red pepper, diced

3 C cold cooked Turkey, chopped

1 C cold dressing/stuffing

1 tsp salt

½ tsp black pepper, ground

½ C sliced almonds

2/3 C gravy or heavy whipping cream

In large, skillet over medium-high heat, place sliced almonds. Stir continually to prevent burning or scorching. Cook until almonds roast, a light, golden brown, or for 2 to 3 minutes. Set aside.

Reduce the heat to medium and melt butter using the same skillet. Add the onions, garlic, and red pepper to the skillet. Sauté, stir constantly until the onions become translucent.

Add in turkey, salt and pepper, and dressing. Mix well. Cook until turkey is thoroughly heated, about 5 minutes.

Add in gravy or cream with the almonds. Cook until all liquid is absorbed, stir frequently, but allowing to sit periodically to toast different areas. Hash will be moist when done, so don't overcook, about 5-10 minutes.

Serve immediately.

Lunch

Turkey-Pasta Soup

Prep Time: 10 min

Cook Time: 10 min

This soup is great as a side dish to sandwiches or can be eaten alone. Using canned broth also speeds the cooking time on this recipe.

Ingredients:

1 Tbsp. olive oil

½ C carrot, chopped

¼ C celery, chopped

¼ C onion, diced

1 garlic clove, minced

2 C water

1/3 C chopped ham

¼ tsp ground black pepper

4 (14-ounce) cans chicken broth

1 C uncooked macaroni

3 C chopped cooked turkey

3 C sliced cabbage

Heat oil in a large saucepan or pot over medium-high heat. Add vegetables (carrot, celery, onion, and garlic). Sauté 3 minutes or until tender. Next, add in the water, ham and broth. Add pepper to taste. Bring to a boil. Add in pasta and cook 8 minutes or until pasta is done. Add in turkey and cabbage; cook 2 minutes more or until cabbage wilts.

Open Turkey-Patty Melt

Prep Time: 10 min

Cook Time: 10 min

Swap your beef for turkey in this delicious melt sandwich. Eat with veggie chips, instead of regular potato chips, for a healthier twist.

Ingredients:

1 tsp olive oil

1 C sweet onion, sliced

¼ C ricotta cheese

1 ½ tsp Worcestershire sauce

½ tsp black pepper

1 lb. ground turkey breast

1 egg white from large egg

4 (1oz) slices Swiss cheese

4 slices bread of preference

¼ C mustard of preference (I like honey with mine)

Heat the oil with the sliced sweet onion in a large skillet over medium heat. Cook until browned slightly, stirring occasionally, about 5 minutes. Remove the onion and place into a bowl, let stand. Preheat your broiler.

Combine all ingredients, except cheese and bread, together. With the ground turkey mixture create four medium-sized patties. Place the skillet back on medium heat. Coat pan with oil or cooking spray and begin cooking patties. Let cook 4 minutes or until browned. Flip and cook the other side. You can add a slice of cheese to the cooking patties after the second side has cooked one minute.

To assemble your toasted melt, place your bread in one layer on the baking sheet and place under broiler. Watch closely and remove when bread is toasted to preference. Cover sides with mustard and then top each slice with one patty. Cover with onion mixture.

Dinner

20 Minute Turkey Chili

Prep Time: 10 min

Cook Time: 20 min

This dish is one that you can eat solo or with rice, spaghetti, over a baked potatoes or with just plain tortilla chips. Try it with scrambled eggs in the morning for a real start to your day!

Ingredients:

1 (3.5oz) bag long-grain rice (boil-in-bag kind)

1 Tbsp. vegetable oil

1 C onion, chopped

3/4 C chopped green bell pepper

½ lb. ground turkey breast

1 Tbsp. chili powder

1 tsp Worcestershire sauce

½ tsp ground cumin

½ tsp dried oregano

¼ tsp salt

¼ tsp black pepper

1 (15oz) can kidney beans, drained and rinsed

1 (14.5oz) can Mexican-style stewed tomatoes, undrained (with peppers and spices, optional)

1 (5.5 oz.) can tomato juice

¼ C (1oz) shredded cheddar cheese

Cook the bag of rice according to package directions. Leave out the salt and butter. While the rice is cooking, get another large skillet to warm over medium-high heat. Toss in the vegetables (onion and bell pepper) and turkey. Cook for 3 minutes until it's done, allow to crumble. Add remaining ingredients except for the cheese. Raise the heat and bring to a boil. Once the chili starts to boil, cover and reduce heat and simmer for another 10 minutes. Remove and serve over the finished rice. Top with the cheese and enjoy!

Turkey Breast in Port Wine

Prep Time: 15 min

Cook Time: 20 min

Stuffing or wild rice make a great side to this delectable dish.

Ingredients:

1 lb. turkey tenderloins

2/3 C beef broth, divided

¼ C port wine

2 Tbsps. chopped dried cherries

2 tsp black cherry fruit spread

1 tsp Worcestershire sauce

½ tsp balsamic vinegar

¼ tsp black pepper

1 tsp cornstarch

1 tsp butter

3 Tbsps. chopped shallots

1 tsp chopped fresh rosemary

Cut tenderloins into slices; try to keep them 1 inch thick. Pound each slice with meat tenderizer or meat shallot until ½ inch thickness is reached. Combine ½ C broth, wine, and the next five ingredients (wine to pepper). In another bowl, combine the remaining broth and cornstarch and stir with a whisk.

Place pan over medium-high heat and melt butter. Add the turkey and cook about 3 minutes. Turn over, and cook 1 minute more. Remove from pan. Now place shallots and rosemary into the pan and cook 3 minutes. Stir constantly. Add the wine mixture now and bring to a boil. Cook 2 minutes more. Now add the cornstarch mixture and boil for more 1 minute. Serve the hot sauce with the turkey and any other side dishes that you have prepared.

Snacks and Desserts

Turkey Salad with Avocado Dressing

Prep Time: 5 min

Cook Time: 0 min

You can prepare this quick and easy meal with roasted turkey from your local deli. The avocado makes a creamy dressing making this simple salad abound in unsaturated fats or omega-3 fatty acids. This recipe makes a nice afternoon snack when you know dinner is ways off.

Ingredients:

¼ C buttermilk

1 Tbsp. mayonnaise

1 Tbsp. lime juice

½ tsp salt

1/8 tsp red pepper (ground or dried flakes)

1 garlic clove, peeled

½ avocado, seeded and mashed loosely

4 C chopped romaine lettuce

2 C roasted turkey breast, diced

½ C green onions, thinly sliced

2 Tbsps. cilantro, chopped

Place the first seven ingredients into a blender and blend until smooth. Make sure you scrape both sides to get all the avocado goodness into your salad. Toss lettuce and remaining ingredients together. Add buttermilk dressing over the lettuce, tossing gently to coat. Serve with sandwiches or toasted French bread with cheese. Enjoy!

Spinach

Breakfast

Spinach-Egg Wrap

Prep Time: 5 min

Cook Time: 5 min

If you were wondering how you could eat spinach for breakfast, now you know! This delicious egg wrap tastes just like a traditional breakfast burrito. You can even add cheese and ketchup!

Ingredients:

½ C baby spinach, chopped

4 eggs

½ tsp salt

¼ tsp pepper

4 oz. pepper jack cheese, shredded

1 avocado, sliced

4 tortillas (strive for whole, unrefined)

Hot sauce or ketchup (optional)

Lightly coat a skillet with oil over medium-high heat. Once the oil is warm, add baby spinach and cook until wilted, about 2 minutes. Meanwhile, whisk the eggs together and cook with spinach until cooked to desired consistency. Keep a little wet to avoid over-cooking, about 3 or 4 minutes. Season to taste with salt and pepper.

Prepare wrap by placing egg and spinach mixture in center of tortilla. Top with cheese, avocado, and fold. Slice in half, if you prefer and serve with ketchup, hot sauce, or salsa.

Cheesy Spinach-Mushroom Breakfast Casserole

Prep Time: 6 hrs. 30 min

Cook Time: 1 hr. 15 min

This breakfast casserole will put your stale bread to tasty use. Because it takes a good amount of time to prep before cooking, prepare this dish the night before and stick in oven first thing in the morning.

Ingredients:

4 Tbsps. olive oil (extra-virgin and then some for cooking)

8 C bread with crust removed and diced into squares

Salt and pepper

4 C Cremini mushrooms, sliced

2 cloves garlic, minced

1 tsp thyme leaves, chopped

5 C baby spinach

4 oz. Gruyere, grated or shredded

1/3 C Parmesan, grated or shredded

8 large eggs

2 ½ C half-and-half

Grease a 3-quart casserole dish with oil. Coat bread cubes in oil, salt and pepper in a large bowl. Now prepare a large skillet, warming over medium heat. Add the moist bread to the skillet and brown, tossing frequently until toasted and brown (8 minutes). Once done, return cooked bread to a bowl to let cool.

Clean out the skillet and add oil to coat over medium-high heat. Add mushrooms, try not to stir immediately. Aim to let the first side truly cook through. When they start to brown, about 3 minutes, begin to stir for another 2 minutes. Now add the garlic, salt and pepper, and thyme, stirring continuously for another minute. Add the spinach with a pinch of salt. Stir often and continue to cook until spinach wilts, about 2 minutes more and then remove from heat.

In the casserole dish, place half the oiled bread cubes, mixing them with half of the Gruyere and Parmesan cheese. Add the mushroom and spinach mixture, topping with the remaining bread cubes, Gruyere, and Parmesan.

In another large bowl, whisk half-and-half together with the eggs, salt, and black pepper. Add to the casserole dish. Let stand covered with plastic wrap, or top that seals and chill for at least six hours or overnight. In the morning, remove the dish and let come to room temperature, about 30 minutes, before baking.

Preheat oven to 350° F. When dish has stood for at least 30 minutes, place in oven, to bake until the top, is set, and the custard is golden brown, 50 to 55 minutes. When finished, remove from oven and let stand at least 15 minutes before cutting to serve.

Lunch

Spinach and Avocado Salad

Prep Time: 5 min

Cook Time: 0 min

Just what it says, this salad can be thrown together in a jiffy. It's tasty, creamy, and healthy!

Ingredients:

1 Tbsp. minced garlic

1 tsp salt

1 lemon (squeezed for taste)

½ tsp mustard (Dijon or honey mustard)

2 Tbsps. extra-virgin olive oil

6 C spinach leaves, loosely packed

1 avocado, cubed

Place garlic into a bowl and whisk with lemon juice, mustard, and a dash of salt. Whip until the salt is dissolved, and then add in oil. Continue to whisk until oil is well blended into the mixture. Set aside and let stand.

Coat spinach leaves with dressing, and then add the cubed avocado. Season with more salt or lemon juice to taste.

Zucchini Rolls, Sun Dried Tomatoes, and Spinach

Prep Time: 5 min (not including seed soak time)

Cook Time: 0 min

Delicious bites of zucchini rolls. It makes a great appetizer and quick lunch on the go!

Ingredients:

For sunflower seeds pate:

1 C sunflower seeds, soaked for 2 hrs.

4 Tbsps. olive oil

2 Tbsps. tahini

4 ½ Tbsps. lemon (squeezed to taste)

1 tsp apple cider vinegar

Pinch of nutmeg

Salt, to taste

Black pepper, to taste

Chili flakes, to taste

For the rolls:

1 large zucchini cut into flat, thin strips (strive for 12)

12 large spinach leaves

12 basil leaves

6 sun dried tomatoes, cut into fine strips

½ C buckwheat (sprouted is best)*

Begin by sprinkling salt onto the strips of zucchini. Let them sit for 5 to 10 minutes. Start on the sunflower seeds by adding all the pate ingredients into a blender. Blend on high until a creamy mix forms. Scoop into a bowl and then season to taste with salt and pepper. Return to the zucchini strips to rinse off any excess salt and then pat dry.

Start on the rolls by taking a slice of zucchini and 1Tbsp of the pate spread. Smooth it over the zucchini slice. Press a tsp of sprouted buckwheat into the pate on the zucchini to keep it from moving around. In the middle, place 2 to 3 sun dried tomato strips, a spinach and basil leaf and then roll up, pinning closed with toothpicks.

Serve immediately. Refrigerate for up to one day, no more.

Notes

*If you don't know how to sprout buckwheat or have any sprouted buckwheat, just substitute using more sunflower seeds or other nut or seed of your preference.

Dinner

Spinach Lentil Over Pasta

Prep Time: 20 min

Cook Time: 1 hr. 15 min

This delicious dish is both filling and healthy! It's a great way to make sure you're getting enough spinach in your diet throughout the week!

Ingredients:

1 small cinnamon stick

¼ onion, peeled

½ onion, minced

½ C dried brown or green lentils

3 ½ tsp salt

½ package jumbo pasta shells (about 20 pieces)

3 Tbsps. olive oil

1 medium carrot, washed, peeled, and diced

1 celery stalk, diced

3 cloves garlic, minced

¼ C red wine

1 sprig thyme or ½ tsp dried

2 ½ C tomato puree

¼ tsp cayenne

Black pepper

4 C spinach, finely chopped

Parmesan cheese for garnish (optional)

Bring 1 cup of water to a rolling boil with the cinnamon stick and ¼ peeled onion. Add the lentils, and then cover, reducing heat to simmer on low. Cook for an additional 25 minutes. Remove the cinnamon and onion and toss in a pinch of salt and stir.

In another large pot, boil 3 quarts of water for the pasta. Add the jumbo shells along with more salt. Cook for 12 minutes; shells will not be completely soft. Drain them and then move to a baking sheet in order to cool and prevent sticking. Spread them out evenly.

In another saucepan, heat oil over medium heat for the vegetables (carrot, minced onion, garlic, and celery). Cook for about 8 minutes, or until soft and tender. Add in tomato puree, cayenne and stir to mix. Cook on low for an additional 10 to 15 minutes. Add the lentils and cook for another 5 to 10 minutes. Salt and pepper to taste. Remove the thyme sprig now, if using fresh. Mix in the spinach and remove from heat, cover.

While it stands heat your oven to 350°F. Coat the bottom of a rectangular or square baking dish with oil. Line up the jumbo shells into the dish. Carefully fill each shell with the ragout mixture. When finished, lavishly cover shells with ragout and cheese, if using. Bake for additional 30 minutes. Remove, let stand to cool, and then serve.

Spinach and Mushroom Bread Pudding

Prep Time: 20 min

Cook Time: 1 hr. 15 min

Pudding for dinner? Not that type of pudding. This dish is jam packed with the nutrients you need to eradicate anxiety from your life while infusing your mouth with incredible taste!

Ingredients:

2 large eggs (or 1 C Egg Beaters egg substitute)

2 C milk (try almond milk)

½ tsp salt

¼ tsp pepper

7 slices bread, cubed (stick with whole grains, wheat, buckwheat, or rye)

10 oz. frozen spinach, thawed

1 Tbsp. olive oil

1 C onion, chopped

1 C red bell pepper, chopped

2 C mushrooms, chopped

½ Tbsp. garlic, minced

1 C Swiss cheese

Preheat oven to 350° and grease an 8x8 cooking pan. Start by whisking together the egg and milk along with salt and pepper. Toss in the bread and then set aside. Squeeze water out of thawed spinach. In a skillet lightly coated with oil on medium heat, add the onion and red pepper. Sauté for 5 minutes and then add the mushrooms and garlic. Do not let the garlic burn, and cook for another 5 minutes. Add the spinach to the skillet and mix, cooking another 5 minutes more.

Add the vegetables along with ½ C cheese to the egg/bread mix and thoroughly combine. Pour the liquid mixture into the greased casserole dish and top with cheese, if using. Bake for 50 minutes, checking the center to be sure egg is cooked thoroughly through. If not, increasing cooking time by 10-minute intervals until done.

Snacks and Desserts

Green Apple Spinach Smoothie

Prep Time: 3 min

Cook Time: 0 min

Tastes better than it sounds!

Ingredients:

Lime

Coconut milk

1 granny smith apple

Baby spinach

Yogurt

Ice cubes

Mint leaves (optional, but I love it for nice zingy freshness!)

For the first layer mix 2 C of spinach ½ C almond milk, 4 ice cubes, and ½ of a chopped Granny Smith apple along with the squeezed juice from one lime into a blender. Blend well and then set aside in a cup for later. Rinse out the blender. Add the almond milk, ½ C of yogurt (organic, Greek or vanilla is delicious), the remaining half of the Granny Smith apple and about 2 to 5 mint leaves. Blend until same consistency as the earlier mixture and add to your cup. Garnish with an apple slice.

Blueberry Spinach Smoothie

Prep Time: 5 min

Cook Time: 0 min

This is another delicious recipe that also calls for blueberry for double the punch of vitamins and minerals that can fight off anxiety. It's great for a mid-meal snack or evening drink when you're craving something sweet, filling, and healthy.

Ingredients:

2/3 C plain Greek yogurt

1 banana

2/3 C blueberries, frozen

2 large frozen strawberries

1 C spinach leaves

½ C milk of choice (try it with almond)

1 Tbsp. of honey, or to taste

Place all ingredients into a blender and cover with the lid. Whirl until smooth, adding more milk to reach your desired consistency. Pour into cups and serve.

Almonds

Breakfast

Almond-Honey Breakfast Bar

Prep Time: 30 min

Cook Time: 5 min

These bars are perfect for you to prepare beforehand and+ grab when you're on the go. Keep the bars at room temperature in order to maintain a soft, chewiness that gets lost if chilled.

Ingredients:

1 C rolled oats

¼ C slivered almonds

¼ C sunflower seeds

1 Tbsp. flaxseeds, preferably golden

1 Tbsp. sesame seeds

1 C puffed cereal (whole-grain)

1/3 C currants

1/3 C dried apricots, chopped

1/3 C chopped golden raisins

¼ C almond butter

¼ C sugar (brown, agave, or another natural sweetener of your choice)

¼ C honey

½ tsp vanilla extract

1/8 tsp salt

Preheat your oven to 350°F. Coat a square pan with butter or cooking spray, set aside. On a baking sheet, get ready to roast your seeds and nuts by spreading out the oats, almonds, sunflower seeds, flaxseeds, and sesame seeds. Bake until you can just begin to smell the nuts, about 10 minutes. Remove and transfer into a large mixing bowl. Add the cereal, currants, dried apricots and raisins and then mix thoroughly.

In a saucepan over low heat, combine the almond butter, sugar, vanilla, and honey. Stir frequently. Cook until the mixture begins to bubble, about 2 to 5 minutes. Remove from heat and immediately pour over the dry ingredients. Mix thoroughly with a spoon. Leave no dry spots. Transfer to your prepared square pan. Press flat. Chill in refrigerator until bar is firm, about 30 minutes, and then cut into even bars.

Chickpea Almond Pancakes

Prep Time: 7 min

Cook Time: 20 min

These pancakes are gluten and grain-free! Perfect for someone watching their carb intake.

Ingredients:

3/4 C almond milk

1 tsp apple cider vinegar

3 Tbsps. maple syrup

2 Tbsps. coconut sugar

1 tsp vanilla extract

¼ tsp almond extract (optional)

¾ C chickpea flour

¼ C almond meal

¼ tsp baking powder

¼ tsp baking soda

1/8 tsp salt

¼ tsp ground cinnamon

In a bowl, mix the almond milk and vinegar together. Let stand for 5 minutes. Then whisk in maple syrup, sugar, vanilla, and almond extract, if using.

In another bowl, mix the chickpea flour, almond meal, baking powder and baking soda with the salt and cinnamon. Once combined, add in the wet mixture and stir until well-blended and smooth. If your batter seems too thick, add more milk or water until desired consistency.

Coat a large skillet with oil or cooking spray and heat over medium heat. Add the batter until hot cake size of preference is reached. Don't put too many hot cakes on the pan that they run together. Cook until top of batter has air vents and appears slightly solid, about 1 ½ minutes depending on the stove top. Flip and cook the other side. About 3 to 5 minutes are total for each hot cake.

Lunch

3.   Flaked Almond "Tuna" Salad

Prep Time: 10 min

Cook Time: 0 min

This vegan dish is more than just meat free. Its rich combination of fresh food and seasonings will give your mouth something it remembers for a long time coming.

Ingredients:

1 cup raw almonds, soaked (at least 3hrs not more than 9)

2 celery stalks, finely chopped

2 green onions, finely chopped

1 garlic clove, minced

3 Tbsps. mayo

1 tsp Dijon mustard

Lemon juice, squeezed to taste

¼ tsp sea salt, to taste

Black pepper, to taste

Pinch of kelp granules (optional)

1 English cucumber, peeled (personal preference) and sliced into 1 cm rounds (optional)

Soak almonds in a bowl of water for 3-9 hours until plump. Drain and rinse well. Add nuts into a food processor or blend and process until they become finely chopped. When finished, it will resemble flaked tuna. Remove almonds and place into a medium mixing bowl.

To the almonds, add the ingredients from the celery to the squeezed lemon juice and mix well. Season with salt and pepper or kelp granules if you want.

To serve, slice the English cucumber into rounds. Carefully scoop out the center of each round to create a small indentation; fill with the almond mixture and position onto platter for serving. If you're not in the mood for cucumber, you can also serve this dish in pita bread, atop a spinach salad or with crackers.

Couscous Salad with Roasted Almonds and Zucchini

Prep Time: 25 min

Cook Time: 10 min

This salad is perfect by itself—but once topped with almonds, it becomes dynamic. Give it a try!

Ingredients:

2 C couscous

1 C fresh peas

1 ½ C finely diced zucchini

6 Tbsps. olive oil

Salt

Black pepper

3 Tbsps. lemon juice, squeezed to taste

2/3 C almonds, chopped (raw is best but you can use roasted)

½ C scallions, sliced

½ C parsley, chopped

¼ C mint, chopped

Crushed red pepper (optional)

Bring 2 C of water to a boil and then pour over couscous. Set aside and let stand for 5 minutes.

Meanwhile, boil peas in ½ C water for only 1 minute. Drain and rinse the peas, keep about ¼ C of the water. In a skillet over medium heat, sauté the zucchini with olive oil to keep from sticking. Cook zucchini about 3 minutes. Season with salt and pepper and set aside to cool at room temperature.

In another bowl, add the saved water from cooking the peas with lemon juice and remaining 3 Tbsps. of olive oil. Add the couscous and fluff. Top with dressing and then stir in the remaining vegetables, nuts, parsley and mint. Season to taste.

Dinner

Creamy Chile-Almond Chicken

Prep Time: 30min

Cook Time: 1hr

Although this recipe calls for tender chicken breasts, it can just as easily be made with turkey to increase the nutrients needed to protect your body from stress and outside stimuli. Try serving with brown or wild rice on the side.

Ingredients:

2 C unsweetened almond milk

½ C chicken broth

¾ C green chilies, chopped and seeded (optional)

3 scallions, sliced with white and green parts separated

3 Tbsps. slivered almonds

1 clove garlic, thinly sliced

Salt

6 chicken breast cutlets or fillets

1 Tbsp. oil

2 Tbsps. whipping cream (optional)

1 Tbsp. sesame seeds, toasted

To begin, combine the almond milk, broth, chilies, whites from the scallions, toasted almonds and garlic in a pot on medium-high heat. Bring to a boil and then reduce heat to low. Simmer the mixture until it is reduced by half, about 20 to 30 minutes. When finished, add to a blender and puree until smooth. Remember to use caution while blending hot liquids.

In a large skillet, heat oil over medium-high heat. Prepare the children by sprinkling with a dash of salt. Add chicken and cook until well browned. Add the sauce and reduce heat to a low simmer, stirring lightly. Cook until chicken is thoroughly done, about an additional 7 minutes. Then remove from heat and place chicken onto a serving platter or plate. If using cream, stir into the sauce now, pouring over the chicken. Garnish with scallion greens and sesame seeds. Serve with a side dish and enjoy!

Almond and Lemon-Crusted Fish

Prep Time: 10 min

Cook Time: 12 min

When you combine fish and nuts, you create an elegant dish, the more so with white fish such as cod and halibut. Get a dose of your omega-3 fatty acids with this tasty fish entree.

Ingredients:

Zest and juice of 1 lemon

½ C almonds, chopped

1 Tbsp. dill, fresh, diced or 1 tsp dried

1 Tbsp. + 2 tsp olive oil, divided

Salt

Black pepper, to taste

1 ¼ lbs. cod or halibut, cut into 4 portions

4 tsp mustard (try Dijon or honey)

2 cloves garlic, thinly sliced

1 lb. baby spinach

Lemon cut into wedges for garnish (optional)

Preheat oven to 400°F. Grease a rimmed baking sheet. Mix the zest with almonds, dill, 1 Tbsp. oil, salt, and pepper in a small bowl. Using the baking sheet, lay the fish out flat, spreading each portion with one tsp of mustard. Now top with the almond mixture, pressing the almonds into the mustard to be sure they stick. Bake until the fish is opaque in the center or 7 to 9 minutes.

Place 2 teaspoons olive oil in a medium saucepan over medium-low heat. Toss in the garlic, stirring lightly to brown, or roughly 30 seconds. Add the spinach, lemon juice and a pinch of salt and pepper. Keep stirring until spinach begins to wilt, about 2 to 4 minutes. Remove from heat and cover to keep warm while fish cooks. Remove the fish from oven when finished and then serve with the spinach and lemon wedges.

Snacks and Desserts

Honey-Almond Cake (Flourless)

Prep Time: 20min

Cook Time: 2hrs

This delicious cake is just the thing for a dessert that is bot healthy and sweet. Try it in the afternoon with tea too.

Ingredients:

1 ½ C whole almonds, toasted

4 large eggs, separated, at room temperature

½ C honey

1 tsp vanilla extract

½ tsp baking soda

Pinch of salt

TOPPING:

2 Tbsps. honey

¼ C sliced almonds, toasted

Preheat oven to 350°F. Grease a 9-inch bread pan. Line the bottom with parchment paper and also grease.

Use processor to break almonds down until extremely fine. Do not process to create a paste. Now take the four egg yolks and beat, mixing in a pinch of salt, honey, vanilla and baking soda. Once thoroughly mixed, add the ground almonds and gently fold into the mixture.

Now take the four egg whites and mix at medium speed with a whisk attachment or a hand-held mixer. If not using a machine, use a whisk and beat till foamy. Don't over beat; whites should not hold peaks. Whisk for about 2 minutes or less.

When doubled in volume, fold the egg whites into the nut batter until just combined. Add to the bread pan.

Bake for about 28 to 30 minutes, or until golden brown; check readiness by inserting a toothpick into the center. It should come out clean without any batter stuck to it. Remove when ready. Keep the cake in pan and let cool for about 10 minutes. To remove, gently loosen sides from pan with a knife and wiggle cake free to let cool completely.

Transfer the cake to a serving platter. Before serving, top the cake with honey and garnish with the silvered almonds.

Salmon

Breakfast

Egg Benedict and Smoked Salmon

Prep Time: 15 min

Cook Time: 15 min

Salmon for breakfast too? Just like spinach and turkey, you'll find that this fish can be enjoyed throughout the day.

Ingredients:

4 eggs

2 Tbsps. white wine vinegar

2 English muffins, halved

Butter (try it with almond)

8 slices smoked salmon

Chives, chopped

For the hollandaise sauce:

2 tsp lemon juice

2 tsp white wine vinegar

3 egg yolks

1 Tbsp. cold butter, diced

To begin, prepare the Hollandaise sauce. Place water into a medium saucepan over medium heat. Let the water simmer. Meanwhile, mix the lemon juice and vinegar in a small bowl. Then add the egg yolks and whisk until frothy. Move the bowl of egg yolks and lemon and vinegar mix to the simmering water and continue whisking until the mixture begins to thicken. Add the butter slowly once sauce begins to thicken, continuing to whisk. If the mixture begins to look like it might be splitting, remove from heat and continue whisking. Season with remaining spices and set aside, covered, to keep warm.

To poach the eggs for the salmon, bring another large pan of water to a boil and add in vinegar. Once boiling, reduce heat to low to allow water to simmer gently. Create a small whirlpool in the pan and slide in the eggs one at a time. Cook egg yolks for about 4 minutes, until solid enough to remove with a slotted spoon.

Meanwhile, toast the muffins. Once eggs are done, remove from pan. Assemble by placing salmon on muffin halves. Top each with an egg and the Hollandaise sauce. Add chopped chives for garnish. Enjoy!

Seared Salmon and Scrambled Eggs

Prep Time: 5 min

Cook Time: 10 min

The fish is great in this egg dish. Eat with your favorite cup of morning coffee or orange juice and some fresh toast for a real morning treat.

Ingredients:

½ Tbsp. butter, plus a couple of pats for spreading

6 large eggs

2 slices sourdough or crusty white bread, griddled or toasted

Salt

Black pepper

4 slices smoked salmon

1 lemon, quartered

Melt ½ Tbsp. of butter in a small saucepan over low heat. Meanwhile, mix the eggs together and add to the saucepan. Prepare to scramble. Use spatula to stir eggs as they cook. Keep a little wet to not overcook and then turn off heat. Prepare your toast with butter and spread of your choosing. Once done, season your eggs to taste with salt and pepper and then add to your toast. Cover with the smoked salmon and serve

lemon juice squeezed from the quartered lemon.
Serve immediately.

Lunch

Orzo and Broiled Salmon

Prep Time: 5 min

Cook Time: 10 min

This dish makes for a hearty lunch, for those who like to eat a little more between breakfast and dinner. Be sure to prepare the orzo beforehand to bring down the lunch preparation time.

Ingredients:

4 oz. uncooked orzo (rice-shaped pasta)

1 ½ tsp olive oil (for pasta)

1 C frozen green peas

4 (4oz) skinless salmon filets

2 Tbsps. Italian salad dressing

2 scallions, thinly sliced (about ¼ C), divided

Preheat broiler and then begin by preparing orzo pasta in a medium saucepan. Use the package directions leaving out directions to season. After 7 minutes of cooking, stir in frozen peas to pasta while it finishes cooking.

While orzo continues cook, place the salmon on a baking sheet covered with foil and greased. Top the filets with salt and the salad dressing. Place under broiler about 4 inches away from the heat and let cook about 6 to 8 minutes, or until center is opaque. Remove and sprinkle about half of the scallions over the salmon.

Set aside pan and attend to orzo. Drain the pasta and peas and return mixture back to the saucepan. Stir in the rest of the scallions and season with salt and pepper to taste. Serve with the salmon.

Dinner

Zucchini and Teriyaki Salmon

Prep Time: 5 min

Cook Time: 15 min

Salmon and zucchini—a wonderful blend of fish and vegetable. Treat yourself to an elegant meal with this recipe.

Ingredients:

Teriyaki sauce

2 (6oz) salmon filets

Sesame seeds

2 small zucchini, sliced thin

4 scallions, coarsely chopped

Oil

Place the filets into a zip-lock plastic bag along with 5 Tbsps. of teriyaki sauce. Seal and let stand to marinate 20 minutes. While marinating, toast the sesame seeds on medium heat in an oiled skillet for about 5 minutes. When done, remove seeds and set aside. Remove the salmon from the marinade and discard the used teriyaki sauce.

In a large skillet add enough oil to coat the bottom of the pan and heat over medium-low heat. Add the fish to the skillet and cook 5 minutes on each side before flipping. Once done, remove from the skillet and set aside to keep warm. Add the zucchini, scallions, and enough oil to coat to your skillet. Sauté, about 4 minutes or until slightly browned. Add in Tbsp. of teriyaki sauce. Sprinkle in sesame seeds and pour over the salmon. Use sesame seeds to garnish as desired.

Skillet Salmon & Potatoes

Prep Time: 8 min

Cook Time: 12 min (30 – 45 minutes more if baking potatoes in the oven)

This meal is quick and easy to prepare. Serve this dinner during the busy time of the week and make sure you family is eating something healthier than fast food.

Ingredients:

1 (6oz) salmon filet

2 medium potatoes

4 Tbsps. grated Parmesan cheese

2 C mixed salad greens

1 C chopped tomatoes

2 Tbsps. balsamic vinaigrette

1 lemon

Salt and pepper to taste

Heat a skillet with a little oil to coat over medium-high heat. Using your hands, coat filet in oil and add to pan to sear. Cook about 6 minutes on each side, or until it begins to flake easily with a fork.

While cooking, prepare potatoes to be cooked in the microwave. Coat potatoes in a light layer of oil and pierce with a fork to allow venting while it cooks. If you don't pierce your potatoes with holes, they will burst while cooking in the microwave. Start potatoes cooking on HIGHEST microwave setting for about 8 to 10 minutes. Turn potatoes after about 5 minutes. Check by piercing potatoes with a fork, they should be soft. Once cooked, remove. If you cook too long in the microwave, potatoes will cool and stiffen. (If you prefer an oven, bake for about 30 – 45 minutes at 350°F).

Cut potatoes in half and season with salt and pepper and cheese, if using. In a bowl, combine the vinaigrette, greens, and tomatoes in a bowl and toss loosely. Squeeze lemon juice over the cooked salmon. Serve with your potatoes and salad and enjoy a deliciously light meal.

Snacks and Desserts

Salmon with Horseradish-Apple Glaze

Prep Time: 3 min

Cook Time: 5 min

Although not quite a snack or dessert, the sweetness from the apple glaze begs to differ. In any case, when you're in the mood for something sweet and savory, this recipe is sure to deliver just what you need!

Ingredients:

1/3 C apple jelly

1 Tbsp. finely chopped fresh chives

2 Tbsps. prepared horseradish

1 Tbsp. champagne vinegar

Salt, to season

4 (6oz) salmon filets (skinned or not is personal preference)

¼ tsp black pepper (fresh is best)

2 tsp olive oil

Preheat oven to 350°. Mix the apple jelly with the chives, horseradish, and vinegar. Mix well with a whisk and add a pinch of salt to taste. Set aside. Prepare the salmon by dusting with a dash of salt and pepper. Heat oil in skillet over medium heat and add salmon, cooking about 3 minutes on each side.

When you turn salmon over, coat the cooked side with some of the apple glaze mixture. Prepare to place whole skillet into the oven by wrapping the handle with foil. Bake for about 5 minutes more or until the fish begins to flake easily with a fork. Remove and top with the remaining apple mixture. Serve with your favorite side dish and enjoy!

Other Natural Ways to Relieve Anxiety

In addition to changing your diet, there are other ways that can help your body better cope with daily stressors from life in general. One key thing, to remember, is that when you're looking to eliminate something from your life completely, it isn't done with a little tweak here and there. Instead, complete healing and change often come from a whole body/lifestyle makeover.

Goal Setting

Anxiety is often compounded or made worse, by the simple fact that we can feel so powerless to change the circumstances causing our distress. That feeling, however real it may be, is still just a feeling. As long as you're alive and breathing, you have options and choices available to you. They just might not be choices you want or are willing to accept. Be that as it may, they're still things you can do.

To help you calm the overwhelming sense of dread and powerlessness, learn how to set goals for yourself throughout life. If you can master this habit, when difficult circumstances come, you'll be able to plan a course of action needed to navigate out of the situation.

Setting goals isn't as easy as you think. Many people say they want something without any plan on how to get it. That's not a goal. It's a dream. Dreams can be upsetting because they're often so big and appear just as overwhelming. They're more daunting than they are inspiring; so many people never advance towards them. That's the danger in dreaming.

To set goals, first, think of short-term accomplishments, things to complete/work towards over the next two to three months. Then think about where you want to be in six months to a year in relationship to the short goals. From there, you can identify long-term goals (things to work towards throughout your lifetime). Learning how to set clear objectives and goals is the first step to learning how to reduce the anxiety caused by life. Just make sure that your goals are S-M-A-R-T:

S – Specific (not a broad statement but something narrow and concrete; I want a part-time job with XYZ Company)

M – Measurable (there must be a way to record the outcome of your specific goal; I want to lose 5 pounds in four weeks.)

A – Achievable (see next)

R – Realistic (achievable and realistic go hand in hand. Your time frame must be achievable and realistic in comparison to your goal. Within my first six months, I want to aim for the first quarter early promotions. I will achieve this by being on time every day, not missing work except for verified excuses, etc.)

T – Timely (for yourself, set a time limit. Your goal will stay measurable and realistic with an honest time of completion. In one year, I plan to move from this department to sales by [insert reasonable actions here])

Daily Exercise

If you're looking to improve your quality of life, unfortunately, it's going to involve exercise. Daily exercise is beneficial to you for so many reasons; it simply can't be ignored any longer. While studies have shown a definite correlation between increased exercise and lowered levels of anxiety and depression, exactly how exercise keeps these two ailments away is unclear. Still, there are several known factors that nearly all studies agree upon:

Endorphins – Things like serotonin and other "feel-good" chemicals are released through physical exercise. Ever hear of the runner's high? It's the same concept.

Raising body temperature – Appears to have a calming effect on brain and thus thoughts and behavior

There are also emotional benefits that are triggered by regular exercise and body maintenance too.

Boost to Confidence – It's no secret: If you're hitting the gym three or more times a week, you're likely going to be in great shape. With the advice from trainers and other regular gym attendees, you just might find yourself becoming a regular health nut addicted to fitness. Talk about a boost to self-image and confidence!

Distraction – When you exercise, the physical exertion can distract you from the unhealthy, negative thoughts caused by anxiety and worry. Working out or playing sports serve as a healthy distraction, which will clear your mind enough to help you think of positive solutions and outcomes to what you're going through.

Breathing Exercises

If you recall, I've listed several times throughout this book that one of the symptoms of anxiety is a speedy heart rate, sweaty palms, and racing thoughts. If left unchecked, these feelings can lead to panic, confusion, and disorientation. Because of this, deep breathing has become a widely recognized, healthy coping mechanism for anxiety and panic. If you slow your breathing, you can manage to regain control of your body, calming it down and taking it out of its fight or flight response.

Deep breathing mimics a portion of our nervous system's maintenance behavior for relaxation. For example, your body continues to breathe, pump blood, and process chemicals while sleeping. The nervous system manages that. It slows heart rate and deepens breathing while resting. Stimulating this system will counteract the portion of the nervous system response to releasing stress hormones when it comes to anxiety.

Conclusion

With as many as 70% of Americans being affected by anxiety to some degree, it's likely that you or someone close to you has struggled with it at some point in their life. It's also possible that you could be struggling with anxiety right now and suffering from a lower quality of life. Controlling your anxiety comes from knowing or understanding how to change the way your body responds to stressful situations.

Just like your life comes with choices that you have to make, you also have the choice to take control of your body and turn it into a healthy, well-functioning machine. You can learn to train your body and mind to handle anxiety and stress better. Find ways to incorporate the five super foods into your diet every day. Make time to decompress after work and do something you enjoy doing. Set realistic goals and reward yourself when you achieve them.

Doing any or all of these things will help you to live a happier, healthier life. After all, isn't that what we all want in the end? And probably the main reason you bought this book in the first place. Remember significant changes do not happen overnight. Don't let a lack of knowledge keep you from living a fully satisfying and rewarding life.

References

1.   http://psychcentral.com/news/2013/06/20/70-percent-of-americans-take-prescription-drugs/56275.html

2.   http://www.nytimes.com/2013/08/20/health/a-dry-pipeline-for-psychiatric-drugs.html?_r=0

3.
        http://www.medicalnewstoday.com/info/anxiety/

4.
        http://www.health.com/health/gallery/0,,20646990,00.html

5.
        http://psychcentral.com/blog/archives/2014/01/02/the-differences-between-normal-worry-general-anxiety-disorder/

6.
        http://www.medicinenet.com/panic_disorder/article.htm

7.   http://www.calmclinic.com/anxiety/how-to-calm-anxiety

8.   http://www.calmclinic.com/anxiety/coping

9.   http://www.mayoclinic.org/diseases-conditions/generalized-anxiety-disorder/expert-answers/coping-with-anxiety/faq-20057987

10.   http://www.prevention.com/health/health-concerns/anxiety-disorders-center/can-certain-foods-affect-my-anxiety

11.   http://www.mayoclinic.org/diseases-conditions/generalized-anxiety-disorder/expert-answers/coping-with-anxiety/faq-20057987

12.   http://chriskresser.com/folate-vs-folic-acid

13.   http://www.mayoclinic.org/diseases-conditions/depression/in-depth/depression-and-exercise/art-20046495

14.
       http://psychcentral.com/blog/archives/2013/07/22/reduce-your-anxiety-this-minute-3-different-types-of-deep-breathing/

15.   http://www.anxietybc.com/self-help/guide-goal-setting

www.ingramcontent.com/pod-product-compliance
Lightning Source LLC
Chambersburg PA
CBHW060952040426
42445CB00011B/1115